The Don't Laugh Challenge ™

12 YEAR OLD EDITION

Don't Laugh Challenge
BONUS PLAY

Join our Joke Club and get the Bonus Play PDF!

Simply send us an email to:

 bacchuspublish@gmail.com

and you will get the following:

- 10 BONUS hilarious jokes!
- An entry in our Monthly Giveaway of a $25 Amazon Gift card!

We draw a new winner each month and will contact you via email!

Good luck!

Welcome to
The Don't Laugh Challenge ™

• How do you play?

The Don't Laugh Challenge is made up of 10 rounds with 2 games in each round. It is a 2-3 player game with the players being 'Jester #1', 'Jester #2', and a 'King' or 'Queen'. In each game you have an opportunity to score points by making the other players laugh.

After completing each round, tally up the points to determine the Round Champion! Add all 10 rounds together to see who is the Ultimate Don't Laugh Challenge Master! If you end up in a tie, use our final Tie Breaker Round for a Winner Takes All!

• Who can play the game?

Get the whole family involved! Grab a family member or a friend and take turns going back and forth. We've also added Bonus Points in game 2, so grab a 3rd person, a.k.a 'King' or 'Queen', and earn an extra point by making them guess your scene!

BILLY BOY

The Don't Laugh Challenge™
Activity Rules

- ## Game 1 - Jokes (1 point each)

  Jester #1 will hold the book and read each joke to Jester #2. If the joke makes Jester #2 laugh, Jester #1 can record a point for the joke. Each joke is worth 1 point. At the end of the jokes, tally up your total Joke Points scored for Jester #1 and continue to Game 2!

- ## Game 2 - Silly Scenarios (2 points each + bonus point)

  Without telling the other Jester what the scenarios say, read each scenario to yourself and then get creative by acting it out! You can use sound effects, but be sure not to say any words! If you make the other Jester laugh, record your points and continue to the next scenario.

  BONUS POINT: Get your parents or a third player, a.k.a King or Queen, involved and have them guess what in the world you are doing! Get the King or Queen to guess the scene correctly and you score a BONUS POINT!

The Don't Laugh Challenge ™
Activity Rules

Once Jester #1 completes both games it is Jester #2's turn. The directions at the bottom of the book will tell you who goes next. Once you have both completed all the games in the round, add your total points from each game to the Round Score Page and record the Round winner!

- ## How do you get started?
  Flip a coin. If guessed correctly, then that Jester begins!

  Tip: Make any of the activities extra funny by using facial expressions, funny voices or silly movements!

ROUND

1

Jokes

What do you call a fortune teller who can fly a plane?

A Palm Pilot.

_____ /1

Did you see that one guy run through the library?

He was really booking it!

_____ /1

What advice do you give to a novice barista?

If at first, you don't succeed, CHAI CHAI again!

_____ /1

Why did the circle hate the scissors?

It was cutting corners!

JOKES TOTAL: _____ /4

JESTER 1 CONTINUE TO THE NEXT PAGE ➡

Silly Scenarios

(Act it out!)

You're trying to sleep, but your right arm has a mind of its own and keeps waking you up! You must fight it off and try to get some sleep!

/2

You are a pro at playing the drums. To you, everything is a possible drum and beat. Get creative and show how you use the world around you as an instrument!

/2

SILLY SCENARIOS TOTAL: _____ /4

 NOW, PASS THE BOOK TO JESTER 2 ➡

Jokes

Why was the seamstress so successful with her clothing business?

/1

Some say that she's a modern-day JEAN-ious!

What did they call Christopher Columbus' journey along the ocean?

/1

A 'Chris'-cross!

Why are computers always getting promotions?

/1

They have a lot of DRIVE!

Why is the Earth so mean?

/1

He's got a bad latitude.

JOKES TOTAL: _____ /4

JESTER 2 CONTINUE TO THE NEXT PAGE ➡

Silly Scenarios

(Act it out!)

Pick an object in the room to auction off and pretend to tell the other player(s) why they should get it! - Remember, only use noises, facial expressions, and exaggerated hand movements. Whenever someone moves, start shouting out random prices until you pick someone and yell, "SOLD!"

/2

While juggling outside, the ground you're standing on is very HOT! Keep juggling while you try to keep your feet cool by jumping, kicking or running around!

/2

SILLY SCENARIOS TOTAL: _____ /4

TIME TO SCORE YOUR POINTS!

JESTER 1

/8

ROUND TOTAL

JESTER 2

/8

ROUND TOTAL

ROUND CHAMPION

ROUND

2

Jokes

What did the glasses say to the face?

"Lens me your ears."

/1

What's a CD's favorite genre of music?

DISK-co, of course!

/1

Why do cups buy houses on the beach?

They always want to be by the coasters.

/1

Why was mama butter so proud of baby butter?

She got On-A-Roll in school. (Honor Roll)

/1

JOKES TOTAL: _____ /4

JESTER 1 CONTINUE TO THE NEXT PAGE ➡

Silly Scenarios

(Act it out!)

You pretend to hold a bottle of lotion and try squeezing it onto your hand. Nothing comes out, so you lift it in the air and peek inside. SUDDENLY, it squeezes right onto your face and in your mouth! EW. Show your best-surprised reaction while wiping it off!

_____/2

You are an itchy cat, that keeps rubbing against the sofa, the wall, ANYTHING to make the itch stop! When your owner walks in, act casual, then go back to itching!

_____/2

SILLY SCENARIOS TOTAL: _____/4

NOW, PASS THE BOOK TO JESTER 2 ➡

Jokes

What did the lobster say to the seaweed?

"I really had to claw my way to the top!"   /1

What do you call it when a mug of tea falls in love with a cup of coffee?

/1

A hot CUP-ple!

Why did the hat quit his job?   /1

He had no head for business.

Why was the grape sad?

/1

He was always WINE-ing.

JOKES TOTAL: _____ /4

JESTER 2 CONTINUE TO THE NEXT PAGE ➔

Silly Scenarios

(Act it out!)

Pretend to start up your chainsaw by tugging on the cord & making noise to indicate it's 'ON'. Start cutting down a tree, but once it's cut you look up to realize it might fall on you! HURRY! Run before it falls in your direction!!

/2

Act like a peaceful flamingo practicing Tai Chi. Remember, elegance is key!

/2

SILLY SCENARIOS TOTAL: _____ /4

TIME TO SCORE YOUR POINTS!

JESTER 1

/8

ROUND TOTAL

JESTER 2

/8

ROUND TOTAL

ROUND CHAMPION

ROUND

3

Jokes

What did the pepperoni say to his wife?

"You'll always be a pizza me. Olive you forever."

/1

Why wouldn't the boat dock at the Marina?

It HARBOR-ed a grudge.

/1

Why did the barge leave the canal?

It felt the tug of the sea.

/1

I overheard the tiger say he was the 'King of the Jungle'... We all know he's lion!

/1

JOKES TOTAL: _____ /4

JESTER 1 CONTINUE TO THE NEXT PAGE ➡

Silly Scenarios

(Act it out!)

Uh oh, you dropped something! Walk down your imaginary stairs by taking tiny steps and dipping your knees with each step, until you're on the floor. Pick up the item, and walk back up your tiny steps until you're full height again!

_____ /2

You're a TV weather person, and there's a GIANT storm coming... but you've lost your voice! Since you can't use words, try to warn the audience about the storm using actions, sounds, and gestures!

_____ /2

SILLY SCENARIOS TOTAL: _____ /4

NOW, PASS THE BOOK TO JESTER 2 ➡

Jokes

What did the grandfather dynamite say at the reunion?

"I'm a real blast from the past!"

/1

What does an owl use to wipe it's face?

A moist t-OWL-ette!

/1

What's a chicken's favorite composer?

Bach Bach Bach!

/1

The horses were being too loud in class, so they were told to REIN it in.

/1

JOKES TOTAL: _____ /4

Silly Scenarios

(Act it out!)

You're getting ready to do the long jump. Warming up with your arms swinging back and forth and knees bent. You take a leap and when you look back, you see that you only jumped a few inches. Act confused and shocked!

___/2

You are trying your best to be quiet an upset newborn baby. You rock it in your arms, burp it, smell it's butt, hold it at arm's length, and eventually, start marking crazy faces to make the baby laugh!

___/2

SILLY SCENARIOS TOTAL: ___/4

TIME TO SCORE YOUR POINTS!

JESTER 1

/8

ROUND TOTAL

JESTER 2

/8

ROUND TOTAL

ROUND CHAMPION

ROUND 4

Jokes

Why are windows so honest?

Because they're always open!

/1

What did the green pepper say to the habanero?

"Wow, you look hot!"

/1

Why did the radio eat dinner at the same time every week?

It wanted to stay on the same frequency!

/1

What do drummers wear to keep the sun out of their eyes?

A high-hat!

/1

JOKES TOTAL: _____ /4

JESTER 1 CONTINUE TO THE NEXT PAGE ➡

Silly Scenarios

(Act it out!)

Pretend you are trying on different glasses. Try on several pairs and pick a character to go with each of them and act like that person. Do the glasses make you look and act cool, nerdy, like a bodybuilder, a supermodel, or an athlete? Get creative and show the crowd!

/2

You have a case of the ultimate burps. Every time you burp, pretend it catapults you backward!

/2

SILLY SCENARIOS TOTAL: _____ /4

NOW, PASS THE BOOK TO JESTER 2 ➡

Jokes

Why is rain so sneaky?

It's always got the drop on people.

/1

Do you know why bread is so thoughtful?

It's always willing to help a friend in knead.

/1

Why did the furniture polish win every race?

He was great at the FINISH!

/1

Where do belly buttons go to school?

The Navel Academy.

/1

JOKES TOTAL: _____ /4

Silly Scenarios

(Act it out!)

Pretend you're Michael Jackson performing on stage in front of thousands of people! They all want to see your most famous moonwalk across the floor. Don't be afraid to add any other funky moves!

/2

While eating a very tasty chicken sandwich, you find a long strand of hair in it. While pulling it out, you realize it might be the longest piece of hair you've ever seen! Give your best-disgusted face and then spit out the pretend sandwich!

/2

SILLY SCENARIOS TOTAL: _____ /4

TIME TO SCORE YOUR POINTS! ➡️

JESTER 1

/8

ROUND TOTAL

JESTER 2

/8

ROUND TOTAL

ROUND
CHAMPION

ROUND
5

Jokes

How do you make a taco stand?

Take away its chair!

/1

Why did the TV want to live in the country?

It wanted a REMOTE location.

/1

What do you get when you cross a man with a seed?

A human bean.

/1

What tool is always fixing their truck?

The screw-DRIVER!

/1

JOKES TOTAL: _____ /4

JESTER 1 CONTINUE TO THE NEXT PAGE ➞

Silly Scenarios

(Act it out!)  **JESTER 1**

You're jogging through the park when a dog quickly comes up behind you and grabs your pants! As you try to get free, pretend your pants completely come off and you freak out! Now chase that dog to get your pants back!

_____ /2

Act like the giant hairdryers that are used in salons. Use your arms to make a circle around someone's head, and blow on their hair. Also, make loud whirring noises to really give it the full effect!

_____ /2

SILLY SCENARIOS TOTAL: _____ /4

 NOW, PASS THE BOOK TO JESTER 2 ➡

Jokes

What's a tailor's favorite saying?

/1

"Keep your friends clothed and your enemies clothier."

Why did the farmer grow tomatoes on his roof?

/1

He wanted his house to have a crop top!

Why can't the shoes dance well?

/1

They've got no SOLE!

What did the basket maker do during rush hour traffic?

/1

He weaved in and out.

JOKES TOTAL: _____ /4

Silly Scenarios

(Act it out!)

Start by doing the 'Hokey Pokey' dance motions. However, every time you put something in the center, act as though it is stuck by what feels to be the world's stickiest glue! Use your whole body to try to pull out your body parts that got stuck, until you just end up completely stuck!

/2

You're a Hollywood stunt double and it's time for the big, slow-motion explosion! Give us your best performance!

/2

SILLY SCENARIOS TOTAL: _____ /4

TIME TO SCORE YOUR POINTS! ➡

JESTER 1

/8
ROUND TOTAL

JESTER 2

/8
ROUND TOTAL

ROUND
CHAMPION

ROUND

6

Jokes

What kind of car concentrates best?

Ford Focus.

/1

How do DJ's steer their cars?

By using turntables.

/1

Why do we never talk about old people's hair?

It's a gray area...

/1

I didn't want to mess up the length, so I bought a quality ruler, just for good measure.

/1

JOKES TOTAL: _____ /4

Silly Scenarios

(Act it out!)

Act like a stalking vulture that is flying in a circle around your prey. When you're ready, try and swoop down to get it! Don't forget your squawk!

/2

You have to make a song using only your body as an instrument. Snap your fingers, slap your legs, tap your feet, and add whatever other noises you can think of to create your musical masterpiece!

/2

SILLY SCENARIOS TOTAL: _____ /4

NOW, PASS THE BOOK TO JESTER 2 ➔

Jokes

Why did the mirror have to re-do his homework?

It didn't **REFLECT** his best work.

_____ /1

How do you get more action and adventure while camping?

When it's in tents!

_____ /1

Why do feet get so confused?

They can never shoes any options!

_____ /1

I never trust the shadows. They always seemed a little shady.

_____ /1

JOKES TOTAL: _____ /4

JESTER 2 CONTINUE TO THE NEXT PAGE ➝

Silly Scenarios

(Act it out!)

Drop down on all fours and pretend you're a lawnmower. While mowing, you accidentally run over a toy and it gets stuck in your gears! Make loud and weird noises to show that you, the lawnmower, are breaking down!

/2

You are an astronaut bouncing around the moon and decide to try to sneak up on the other astronauts, but are moving **SUPER SLOW** due to anti-gravity!

/2

SILLY SCENARIOS TOTAL: _____ /4

TIME TO SCORE YOUR POINTS! ➔

JESTER 1

/8

ROUND TOTAL

JESTER 2

/8

ROUND TOTAL

ROUND CHAMPION

ROUND
7

Jokes

How many lawns did the boy mow in the 3x3 neighborhood?

The whole nine yards!

/1

What did the wife tell her husband, after their child was delivered?

"She's beautiful. It's no wonder since she resembles ME!"

/1

Why did the blanket get impeached?

He was guilty of a cover-up!

/1

What do you use to clean your trumpet?

A tuba cleaner!

/1

JOKES TOTAL: _____ /4

JESTER 1 CONTINUE TO THE NEXT PAGE ➞

Silly Scenarios

(Act it out!)

Act like a cowboy that is ready to draw! Act like you're doing a shoot-off, but instead, start sketching!

/2

You are an **EXTREME CHEF!** Bake, fry, stir, pour, and do a bunch of other kitchen-related actions while wearing an angry face and screaming hard-core. Channel your inner Gordon Ramsey!

/2

SILLY SCENARIOS TOTAL: _____ /4

NOW, PASS THE BOOK TO JESTER 2 ➔

Jokes

JESTER 2

Why didn't the french fry forgive her boyfriend for forgetting their anniversary? ___/1

She was too salty.

What do you call naive candy? ___/1

Suckers.

What do you call a sea creature with a bad attitude? ___/1

Crabby!

What do you get when you cross a Shaman and a horse? ___/1

A s-HORSE-erer.

JOKES TOTAL: ___/4

JESTER 2 CONTINUE TO THE NEXT PAGE

Silly Scenarios

(Act it out!)

You are a Matador in the big stadium, starring down a huge bull. Act out the duel using evasive movements and the whoosh of your cape! Dodge and move as the bulls run towards you!

/2

You are performing a play on the theatre stage, but it is SO slippery! Show the world your slippery, silent play!

/2

SILLY SCENARIOS TOTAL: _____ /4

TIME TO SCORE YOUR POINTS!

JESTER 1

/8

ROUND TOTAL

JESTER 2

/8

ROUND TOTAL

ROUND CHAMPION

ROUND
8

Jonkes

What did the muscle say to the artery?

"You're so vein."

/1

What does a detective say when they don't have any leads?

"I haven't got a CLUE!"

/1

Why was the map such a fast dresser?

He always knew what to WHERE!

/1

Which maid got the new job?

The one with the cleanest record!

/1

JOKES TOTAL: _____ /4

JESTER 1 CONTINUE TO THE NEXT PAGE ➜

Silly Scenarios

(Act it out!)

You're stuck in an elevator and suddenly have the urge to use the restroom. You cross your legs and do the "I need to go **NOW**" dance, while you keep pushing the button to try and get it to go faster. **FINALLY**, it opens and you run!!!

_____ /2

Oh wow, those are some really nice shoes you got on! While your hands are by your sides, do a fun two-step, putting one foot in front of the other tapping your toes from side to side, to show off your new kicks!

_____ /2

SILLY SCENARIOS TOTAL: _____ /4

 NOW, PASS THE BOOK TO JESTER 2 ➡

Jokes

What did the penguin say to the walrus?

"I guess we go with the floe."

/1

Why was the button late?

It kept getting pressed for time!

/1

What did the roller say to the paint?

"I love your new coat."

/1

What do vegan cowboys wear?

Fruit Leather.

/1

JOKES TOTAL: /4

Silly Scenarios

(Act it out!)

You're pulling the petals off a flower as you think "he loves me, he loves me not". As you get to the last petal of the flower, the flower grows more petals! You're shocked and throw the flower on the ground, stomp all over it, and walk away with your nose in the air!

___/2

Become the inflatable noodle man you see outside of car dealerships and dance!

___/2

SILLY SCENARIOS TOTAL: _____ /4

TIME TO SCORE YOUR POINTS! →

JESTER 1

/8

ROUND TOTAL

JESTER 2

/8

ROUND TOTAL

ROUND
CHAMPION

ROUND
9

Jokes

What did the geologist name his daughter?

Crystal.

_____ /1

How do you calm down a big storm?

You have to look them in the eye.

_____ /1

Why didn't anyone trust the shoe?

It was always being a heel.

_____ /1

Why did the teacher drink orange juice instead of apple juice?

It gave her more concentration.

_____ /1

JOKES TOTAL: _____ /4

Silly Scenarios

(Act it out!)

You're lifting a huge barbell. You get it above your head, but suddenly your pants rip at the same time (make a loud ripping noise)! You drop the weight and walk sideways, covering your back to hide the rip! Don't forget to show your most embarrassed face!

/2

You are in a hurry, but you have to run on a slippery surface. Show us how hard it is to keep your balance and still get there on time!

/2

SILLY SCENARIOS TOTAL: _____ /4

 NOW, PASS THE BOOK TO JESTER 2 →

Jokes

My shoes got fed up with me and said they're not letting me walk all over them anymore.

_/1

What do you call a dime a dozen?

$1.20

_/1

How much room did the chef need to cook in?

This MUSHroom!

_/1

What's the ocean's favorite dessert?

Shell-O!

_/1

JOKES TOTAL: _____ /4

JESTER 2 CONTINUE TO THE NEXT PAGE ➡

Silly Scenarios

(Act it out!)

You're sleeping when you suddenly get up and start sleepwalking. As you're sleepwalking you start to pretend smacking yourself in the face, then someone splashed you with water! You wake up out of your sleepwalking and saw that you were completely drenched, but since you're confused you just go back to sleep.

/2

Act like a big seal that is flapping around and doing yoga moves!

/2

SILLY SCENARIOS TOTAL: _____ /4

TIME TO SCORE YOUR POINTS! ➡

JESTER 1

/8

ROUND TOTAL

JESTER 2

/8

ROUND TOTAL

ROUND CHAMPION

ROUND
10

Jokes

Why did the Fashion Police do such a good job?

They always put people under a vest.

/1

How did the calendar feel after Friday?

Like a WEAK-end.

/1

What meal is it when an Italian person leaves?

Ciao Time.

/1

Why was the writer trapped inside?

Because of a rough draft.

/1

JOKES TOTAL: _____ /4

 JESTER 1 CONTINUE TO THE NEXT PAGE →

Silly Scenarios

(Act it out!)

It's time to rise and shine! You wake up yawning to find that your bed is now a boat and you're floating away! You'll need to paddle it back to shore with your hands, but don't fall over!

/2

Give your best impression of a vampire who's been exposed to the sunlight for the first time!

/2

SILLY SCENARIOS TOTAL: _____ /4

 NOW, PASS THE BOOK TO JESTER 2 ➡️

Jokes

What did the bean do for work?

He was a TOOTER! (Tutor)

/1

Why is orange juice a good mentor?

It always says 'Concentrate'!

/1

Knock Knock!
Who is it?
It be!
It be, who?
It behooves you to let me in!

/1

What do you call a unicorn with a bad attitude?

/1

A Uni-SCORN!

JOKES TOTAL: _____ /4

 JESTER 2 CONTINUE TO THE NEXT PAGE ➡

Silly Scenarios

(Act it out!)

As you ice skate across the floor, you also decide to play your favorite song on the violin. Make sure you do both at the same time!

/2

Act like a confused frog, who can't stop jumping backward!

/2

SILLY SCENARIOS TOTAL: _____ /4

TIME TO SCORE YOUR POINTS! →

JESTER 1

/8

ROUND TOTAL

JESTER 2

/8

ROUND TOTAL

ROUND CHAMPION

ADD UP ALL YOUR POINTS FROM EACH ROUND.
THE PLAYER WITH THE MOST POINTS IS CROWNED
THE ULTIMATE LAUGH MASTER!

IN THE EVENT OF A TIE, CONTINUE TO THE ROUND
11 FOR THE TIE-BREAKER ROUND!

JESTER 1

_____
GRAND TOTAL

JESTER 2

_____
GRAND TOTAL

_____

THE ULTIMATE
DON'T LAUGH CHALLENGE MASTER

ROUND

11

TIE-BREAKER

(WINNER TAKES ALL!)

Jokes

Why did the scarf and mitten get along?

They had a common thread.

/1

What did the ball say to the cat?

"Are you feline playful today?"

/1

What type of food do mobsters like to eat?

Take-out.

/1

Why was the King always drinking?

When he reigns, he pours!

/1

JOKES TOTAL: _____ /4

Silly Scenarios

(Act it out!)

You are a person who signals aircraft on and off the runway. Your favorite way to do this is the krumping dance style! Now get that plane to take off! (Krumping is a dance style that uses lots of expressive movement)

/2

You are a psychic looking into a crystal ball. Wave your hands around the imaginary ball and then put your fingers to your temples as you recite a chant of gibberish and try to read the future!

/2

SILLY SCENARIOS TOTAL: _____ /4

 NOW, PASS THE BOOK TO JESTER 2

Jokes

What do you call a noisy mermaid?

A Siren.

/1

What do you call a cool plate?

A RAD-dish.

/1

Why did the puddle dry up?

It's reign was over.

/1

What did the horse name his son?

Neigh-than.

/1

JOKES TOTAL: _____ /4

JESTER 2 CONTINUE TO THE NEXT PAGE ➡

Silly Scenarios

(Act it out!)

Motorcycle obstacle course! You have to go through tunnels, over jumps, do figure eights, and come to a sliding halt. Ready...GO!

/2

Show your talent as the World's Greatest Bowler. However, your legs don't bend at the knees nor do your arms bend at the elbow. Your arms and legs must be completely straight as you show off bowling at its best.

/2

SILLY SCENARIOS TOTAL: _____ /4

TIME TO SCORE YOUR POINTS!

ADD UP ALL YOUR POINTS FROM THE PREVIOUS ROUND. THE JESTER WITH THE MOST POINTS IS CROWNED THE ULTIMATE DON'T LAUGH CHALLENGE MASTER!

JESTER 1

/8
_____
GRAND TOTAL

JESTER 2

/8
_____
GRAND TOTAL

_____

THE ULTIMATE
DON'T LAUGH CHALLENGE MASTER

Check out our

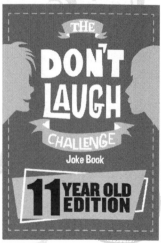

Visit us at
www.DontLaughChallenge.com
to check out our newest books!

other joke books!

If you have enjoyed our book, we would love for you to review us on Amazon!

Made in the USA
San Bernardino, CA
16 November 2019